DE TO THE SACRED HEART

"Take up my yoke upon you, and learn of me, because I am meek, and humble of heart: and you shall find rest to your souls."
—Matthew 11:29

The Sacred Heart is our King,
Our Friend and Confidant, our Counselor.

DEVOTION TO THE SACRED HEART

INCLUDING
THE GREAT PROMISE OF THE
NINE FIRST FRIDAYS

"My son, give me thy heart."
—Proverbs 23:26

TAN Books
Charlotte, North Carolina

Nihil Obstat: ✠ Stephanus Schappler, O.S.B.
            Abbas Coadjutor Im. Conceptionis

Imprimatur: ✠ Carolus Hubertus Le Blond
            Episcopus Sancti Josephi

Originally published at Clyde, Missouri, under the title *True Veneration of the Sacred Heart*. 8th Edition, November, 1949; 135,000. "All rights reserved." Retypeset and republished by TAN Books in 2010.

ISBN: 978-0-89555-902-9

Cover design: Sebrina Higdon

Cover image: Stained glass window, St. Ann Church, Charlotte, North Carolina. Photo © Lauren A. Rupar.

Printed and bound in the United States of America.

TAN Books
Charlotte, North Carolina
2010

"ANNOUNCE it, and let it be announced to the whole world, that I set neither limit nor measure to My gifts of grace for those who seek them in My Heart!"

—Our Lord to
St. Margaret Mary Alacoque

Contents

The Author of This Booklet

Although it bears no author's name, this booklet is likely to have been written by the Servant of God Fr. Lukas Etlin, O.S.B. (1864-1927), saintly chaplain of the Benedictine Sisters of Clyde, Missouri. (See Chapter 43 of *Modern Saints—Book One*, by the late Ann Ball.)

Through a printing apostolate operated by the Benedictine Sisters, Fr. Lukas Etlin labored zealously to spread devotion to the Sacred Heart and adoration of the Holy Eucharist among the lay faithful, not just among priests and religious. He worked with Fr. Mateo Crawley-Boevey, CC.SS. (1875-1960), the famous apostle of the Sacred Heart of Jesus. (See chapter 44 of *Modern Saints—Book Two* and pp. 45-48 of this booklet.)

Fr. Etlin was originally from Switzerland. From his Benedictine community in America he initiated and ran the *Caritas* program, which raised millions of dollars after World War I for destitute seminarians in ravaged Europe.

An artist, Fr. Etlin painted some of the beautiful frescoes at Conception Abbey in Conception, Missouri.

Fr. Etlin died in a car accident in 1927. He was found with a piece of his rosary clutched tightly in his hand. Earlier that day he had told a class of school girls: "We must at all times be ready to die. We should not wish to live even a single day longer than God wills. Should death overtake us in an automobile, also then we should accept it with resignation to the Will of God."

Fr. Lukas Etlin is the author of the popular TAN booklet entitled *The Holy Eucharist—Our All*, which was also formerly published by the Benedictine Sisters of Clyde, Missouri. Readers will find the same saintly spirit and priestly authority in the present work.

DEVOTION
TO THE
SACRED HEART

"*My heart hath expected reproach and misery. And I looked for one that would grieve together with me, but there was none: and for one that would comfort me, and I found none.*"
—Psalm 68(69): 21

Chapter 1

True Devotion to the Sacred Heart

Heart of Jesus, Symbol of Love

THE Church, governed and taught by the Holy Ghost, has approved and recommended devotion to the Sacred Heart of Jesus and has enriched it with many indulgences. She has instituted the Feast of the Sacred Heart, which, in the course of years, has increased in extent and solemnity until now it is celebrated solemnly with an octave by the universal

1

Church on the Friday after the Octave of Corpus Christi.

Confraternities have been established, and throughout the Christian world numberless altars, chapels and churches have been dedicated to the Sacred Heart. Through the Apostleship of Prayer, millions of the faithful daily offer all their prayers, works and sufferings for the intentions of the Sacred Heart of Jesus. During the past two hundred years or more, the Popes have zealously employed their sovereign power in fostering devotion to the Sacred Heart. Pope Leo XIII, toward the end of his long pontificate, consecrated the whole human race to the Sacred Heart. Thus the Church has, as it were, earnestly *forced* this devotion upon us. Zealously to promote the Sacred Heart devotion means to work in the Spirit of God, who ordains that at all times the Church should adopt *just that devotion which is of most profit to her,* because the Holy Spirit knows the needs of the times and the remedies for the times.

In our age of religious indifference, when fervor and charity have grown cold, Jesus exhibits to the world His Sacred Heart as the symbol of God's infinite love—the symbol of His own generous self-sacrificing love for men. Jesus shows His Divine Heart as a furnace whose burning rays of love are able to reanimate faith and rekindle love in hearts grown cold and ungrateful.

But why His *Heart?* Because in every language, in every age, the heart is regarded as the natural symbol of love and affection. What more natural and expressive symbol is there, then, of the excessive love of Jesus than His Sacred Heart?

The *direct* and *material object* of devotion to the Sacred Heart is the *real, physical Heart* of Jesus—the Heart of flesh, the living and loving Heart of our Blessed Lord; the Heart that beat in His Divine breast at the moment of the Incarnation; the Heart that loved us during the life of Jesus on earth, that poured forth Its blood to the last drop on Mount Calvary; the beatified Heart now glorious in Heaven and still dwelling among us in the Blessed Sacrament; the Heart ever united to the Person of the Divine Word, to whom is due supreme homage and adoration.

Besides the direct and material object of the devotion, there is another, called the *spiritual* object, and that is the infinite charity or love of Jesus Christ, of which His Sacred Heart is a symbol. The substance of devotion to the Sacred Heart really consists in calling to mind and in venerating the unbounded charity and excessive love of our Redeemer under the symbol of His Heart.

In 1765 Pope Clement XIII, when granting permission to the Order of the Visitation for the observance of the Feast of the Sacred Heart, expressed the wish that the faithful in celebrating this feast should "call to mind the principal benefits received from the love of Jesus: 1st, in assuming our nature (His Incarnation); 2nd, in suffering and dying for our Redemption (His Passion); and 3rd, in instituting the Sacrament of His Body and Blood (the Holy Eucharist)."

By this devotion, Holy Church desires to reveal to the faithful the most holy affections, desires and movements of the Sacred Heart, through which our Saviour honored His Heavenly Father, sanctified the faithful and presented Himself to mankind as the perfect model of eminent sanctity. These emotions of the Heart of Jesus are: a burning zeal for the glory of His Father, a boundless love for all mankind, a most profound humility, an unconquerable patience, a total sacrificing and devoting of self to the will of the Father, a perpetual adoration of God's sovereign Majesty, an unceasing act of thanksgiving, etc. All these emotions and affections were present even at the first moment of His Incarnation; they animated His Heart to the last moment on the Cross and will continue to animate His Heart in the Blessed Sacrament to the end of time.

Chapter 2

Motives Impelling Devotion

BY Original Sin man lost Sanctifying Grace and thereby forfeited the right to Heaven. But God, in His merciful love, had decreed from eternity to restore him to the state of supernatural grace and to make him worthy of eternal happiness. This was to be accomplished by the *Incarnation of the Son of God,* who, in place of the fallen human race, would render perfect satisfaction to Divine Justice.

Accordingly, in the fullness of time the Eternal Son of God became man, by the power of the Holy Spirit, assuming human nature in the womb of the virginal Mother, Mary. In the mystery of the Incarnation, the Divine and human natures were inseparably united in the Second Person of the Blessed Trinity, in the "hypostatic" union. By virtue of the hypostatic union of the two natures, it follows that all the actions and all the sufferings of Jesus Christ are of infinite worth and merit because they are deeds of a God Incarnate and are referred to the Divine Person.

Redemption began with the Incarnation, and the first act of homage and love of the Incarnate God ascended to Heaven to the Eternal Father from the blessed Heart of Jesus which throbbed in Mary's womb.

Love of the Sacred Heart In the Redemption

For 30 years the Incarnate Word of God was hidden and almost unknown. True, His Immaculate Mother, St. Joseph and a few other favored ones knew Him and returned love for love to His Divine Heart, but outside of this little circle, Jesus was not known. Yet His mercy embraced the whole world; sweet love and holy, silent reparation ascended to Heaven at every moment, day and night, from His Sacred Heart to appease the just wrath of the Eternal Father.

The entire life of Jesus Christ on earth had no other object than the *Redemption and restoration of the human race.* It was a life of abasement in His Incarnation, in His birth and in His hidden and public life, which terminated in His Passion and Death. By the agonizing tortures and most profound humiliations of His Passion, and especially by His Death on the Cross, Jesus became our Redeemer who rendered *superabundant satisfaction* for our sins. Even though the sins of mankind are almost infinite in number and enormity, and an infinite offense against God, yet the Life, Passion and Death of the God-man have made *perfect reparation for these offenses.* He was able to do this in our stead because He is our *Head* and we are His members, and whatever He has done in satisfaction for our sins will be considered by God *as though we ourselves had done it.* Still, we must not forget that despite this perfect and superabundant satisfaction, the gift of the Death of Christ will be beneficial only to those *to whom the merit of His Passion is applied, only to those who cooperate with the graces of Redemption.* These are applied principally through the holy Sacraments, whereby Sanctifying Grace is either imparted to us or increased.

What gratitude, what love, what thanksgiving we owe to the Divine Heart of Jesus for these inestimable benefits for our salvation! Oh, let us praise and love that blessed Heart which at every pulsation sent the Precious Blood through the veins of our Saviour during the whole course of His earthly life; that loving Heart which broke with anguish on the Cross for our Redemption; that Heart which, in the Blessed Sacrament, is always present, really, truly and living, and which has ever loved us and desires to love us eternally; that Heart which is the source of all graces, the seat and center of the infinite and incomprehensible love of Jesus Christ for all mankind.

Love of the Sacred Heart In the Blessed Sacrament

The sufferings and death of our Divine Redeemer on the Cross did not satisfy the love of His Sacred Heart. When about to ascend to His Heavenly Father, His infinite power and wisdom invented a means by which He might be in Heaven with His Father and at the same time remain on earth with His beloved children. *The Blessed Eucharist is this Divine invention.*

It was the last and greatest expression of the burning love of the Sacred Heart of Jesus before His Passion. It was His last legacy to us in fulfillment of His promise not to leave us orphans.

In the Blessed Sacrament, Jesus Christ is *really, truly and substantially present,* with His Body and Blood, with His Soul and His Divinity. He is personally present, not by a mere sign or image, not in a spiritual manner only.

Devotion to the Sacred Heart, as expressly declared by the Sacred Congregation of Rites, *is essentially the same as devotion to the Blessed Sacrament.* It honors the Divine love of our Eucharistic God which revealed itself in His Passion and Death and continually reveals itself in the Holy Eucharist. Therefore, the Sacred Heart devotion is the most agreeable to Our Lord in the Blessed Sacrament.

In fact, the revelations of saints prove that Jesus wishes devotion to His Divine Heart to be inseparably connected with the Blessed Sacrament. In the following touching words He spoke to St. Gertrude of the love of His Sacred Heart in the Holy Eucharist: "My delights are to be with the children of men. To satisfy My love I have obliged Myself to remain therein even to the end of the world, and I wish It [the Holy Eucharist] to be frequently received. Should anyone deter a soul in the state of grace from Communion, he would impede the delight of My Heart. *I have done My utmost to manifest the tenderness of My Heart in the Blessed Eucharist.*"

The revelations of the Sacred Heart to St. Margaret Mary also show most clearly that the Divine Heart wishes this devotion to be practiced in connection with devotion to the Holy Eucharist. About 70 revelations to St. Margaret Mary have been handed down to us, and the greater number of these proceeded from the Sacred Host in the tabernacle. The solemn reparation which Our Lord desires, He asks in satisfaction for the insults offered to Him in the Sacrament of His Love.

Oh, the infinite love of the Sacred Heart of Jesus dwelling day and night on our altars! This love has compelled Him to abide in hundreds of thousands of tabernacles and to remain with us till the end of time.

If we are animated by a true devotion

to the Sacred Heart, we shall feel urged to visit Our Lord in the tabernacle frequently. With a living faith we shall adore Him in the Blessed Sacrament, wherein He pours out the riches of His Divine love for men; wherein He Himself is present, really, truly and substantially, with Divinity and Humanity, with Soul and Body, under the appearance of bread—living, immortal and glorious.

On the altar He dwells among us with His Heart full of love; He abides with us all the days to the end of time, like a father with his children, to aid and console us in need and difficulty; to strengthen, guide and lead us as He did His disciples during His earthly life. Oh, let us then go to the tabernacle with reverence and love and there confidently pour out to Him our hearts, thank Him for all His gifts, implore His forgiveness for our sins and shortcomings and lay before Him our needs and desires, our hopes and longings.

Love of the Sacred Heart in the Holy Sacrifice of the Mass

The Holy Eucharist is not only a Sacrament, it is also a *sacrifice*. On the altar, as on Calvary, Jesus is immolated, and the Precious Blood of His Sacred Heart is mystically separated from His Body. Holy Mass is the true and perfect Sacrifice of the New Law instituted by Christ. In its essence the Sacrifice of the Mass is not different from the Sacrifice of the Cross: *it is one and the same Sacrifice;* the *Oblation* and the *sacrificing Priest are the same* as in the Sacrifice of the Cross. Only the manner of offering is different, because on the Cross Christ offered Himself in a *bloody manner,* while in Holy Mass He offers Himself in an *unbloody manner.* The Sacrifice of the Mass is the most *perfect sacrifice of praise and adoration,* the most *sublime sacrifice of thanksgiving,* the most *efficacious sacrifice of propitiation* and the most *powerful sacrifice of supplication.*

The Sacrifice of the Mass, like that of the Cross, is of infinite worth and infinite efficacy. It increases Sanctifying Grace in the just, expiates venial sins and temporal punishment of sin and gives strength to do what is good. For sinners, the Sacrifice of the Mass effects the grace of contrition and conversion, so that in the Sacrament of Penance (Confession) they may again become reconciled with God. Through the Sacrifice of the Mass we also obtain the protection of God in temporal dangers and aid in afflictions.

Behold the infinite love of the Sacred Heart in the most adorable Sacrifice of the Mass! No wonder St. Bonaventure says, "The Mass is a compendium of all God's love for men"; and St. Francis de Sales calls the Mass ". . . a mystery which comprises the *entire abyss of Divine love.*" Love for the Divine Heart will prompt us to assist at the Sacrifice of the Mass frequently—daily, if possible. Ah, were there but one priest on earth, were the Holy Sacrifice offered in one place only, how we would flock to that priest, to that privileged spot on earth, in order to participate in the mysteries of Divine love! O Sacred Heart of Jesus, inspire us with faith, love and reverence for Holy Mass.

Love of the Sacred Heart In Holy Communion

We have spoken of the infinite love of Jesus in dwelling on our altars, but who can fathom His boundless love in becoming our spiritual food! To nourish and fortify souls, our Blessed Lord gives nothing less than His own adorable Body and Blood. "The bread that I will give," says the Redeemer, "is My Flesh for the life of the world." (*John* 6:52). Christ has expressly commanded the faithful to receive It. He has even made the reception of the Holy Eucharist a condition for attaining life everlasting. "Amen, amen, I say unto you, unless you eat the Flesh of the Son of Man and drink His Blood, you shall not have life in you." (*John* 6:54).

In Holy Communion the Blood of the Sacred Heart of Jesus flows upon the soul to wash away its [venial] sins and to impart to it strength and courage to walk with fortitude on the way to the Kingdom of Heaven. An effect of devotion to the Divine Heart will be the desire frequently to approach the Holy Table, where Love Divine impels the Sacred Heart of Jesus to become our food, to enter our hearts and to unite His Heart with ours. Yes, in Holy Communion we become *one heart and soul* with the Heart of Jesus; here our heart reposes on the Heart of Jesus in a most holy and intimate union; here our soul is filled with the virtues and graces of this

Divine Heart; here our whole being is incorporated with God Himself; here our heart is filled with heavenly bliss, and the germ of a glorious resurrection is implanted in us. O Sacred Heart of Jesus, fill our souls with love for Thee in Holy Communion!

Love Demands a Return of Love

Every pulsation of the Sacred Heart of Jesus, from the first moment of the Incarnation to Its last throb on the Cross, was for purest love of mankind. True devotion to the Sacred Heart demands that we love Him in return, for love demands *a return of love.*

If you truly love the Heart of Jesus, you will take delight in going often to the house of God, where the perpetual light ever glows before the tabernacle. If you love the Heart of Jesus, you will take delight in kneeling often before the altar, where, in the Holy Sacrifice of the Mass, your Saviour mystically renews in an unbloody manner His death upon the Cross. If you love the Heart of Jesus, you will often and devoutly approach the Holy Table. If you love the Heart of Jesus, you will endeavor not to grieve It by sin, especially not by mortal sin.

Our Lord's object in revealing devotion to His Sacred Heart is to draw us to make a return for His love. Yes, He has singled it out among a multitude of other ways and calls it a "species of new Redemption" as a means to renew the world in these latter times. In the 13th century He revealed to St. Gertrude that this devotion was "reserved for latter times, that the time-worn world, grown cold in the love of God, might be warmed up by hearing of such mysteries."

Four centuries later, He complained in sorrowful accents to St. Margaret Mary Alacoque, the confidante of His Eucharistic abandonment: "Behold this Heart which has loved men so much that It spared no sacrifice, not even death and annihilation, in order to testify to them Its love. And in return I receive from the greater part of mankind only ingratitude, by reason of the contempt, irreverence, sacrilege and coldness which they show Me in this Sacrament of Love. This I feel more keenly than all I endured in My Passion. If they would answer love for love, I would look upon all I have done for them as little, and I would, if that were possible, do still more. But they meet My eagerness to do them good only with coldness and rebuffs. Do thou at least give Me the consolation of supplying for their ingratitude, as far as thou art able."

Conscious of His infinite love, can we refuse Jesus the return of love for which He longs? Ah, no!

We will show Thee our love and gratitude, O Sacred Heart of Jesus, by keeping Thy sacred precepts, by rendering Thee atonement and reparation, by honoring the image of Thy Divine Heart and by confiding in Thine all-powerful assistance.

Chapter 3

True Devotion
and Atonement

TRUE devotion to the Sacred Heart demands, further, *reparation* and *atonement*. If you truly love the Heart of Jesus, you will grieve that this Divine Heart is so little loved, so often forgotten, reviled, grieved and offended, and you will grieve in particular at the infidelity, the ingratitude and the outrages that are committed against this loving Heart in the Most Blessed Sacrament.

When we are sad and lonely and discouraged, how much do we not appreciate the compassion of a sympathetic friend! When a person shares another's grief, it loses half its intensity. Such consolation we give to the Divine Heart of Jesus whenever we render reparation for the ingratitude heaped upon It. Our Lord desires this atonement, this sympathy so much that He entreated St. Margaret Mary, saying: "Do thou at least give Me this consolation, and endeavor, as far as lies in thy power, to make atonement for the ingratitude of men."

The Communion of Reparation

This return of love, this atonement, so pleasing to Our Lord, is rendered especially by the Communion of Reparation. In Holy Communion Our Lord gives you a gift of infinite worth, the greatest and best that Heaven and earth possess: He presents *Himself* to you as food of your soul. The most beautiful blossom of devotion to the Sacred Heart is the Holy Communion that you receive to please Our Lord and make atonement—*the Communion of Reparation.*

Once, on the Feast of St. John the Apostle, Our Lord appeared to St. Margaret Mary and made known to her that the devotion to His Sacred Heart was, as it were, the last effort of His love to save mankind. He said that by this devotion He desired to annihilate the dominion of sin in the hearts of men and to establish in its place the dominion of love. In no way is this twofold purpose accomplished more perfectly than by the frequent and worthy reception of Holy Communion.

Our Lord frequently complained to St. Margaret Mary of the indignities and irreverences offered to His Heart when exposed upon the altars. "I have a burning thirst," He said, "to be honored by men in the Blessed Sacrament, and I find scarcely anyone who strives according to My desire to allay this thirst by making Me some return." Would to God it were only heretics and infidels who wound the Sacred Heart of Jesus in the Blessed Sacrament! But alas, it is Catholics who do not love our Saviour—His special, privileged friends of the sanctuary, chosen spouses, who offer Him a divided heart; and this ingratitude of His *friends* gives more pain to His Divine Heart than the insults of His *enemies*.

Catholics believe and know that in their midst is their God, their Redeemer, their Judge, their All; but do they *love* Jesus? Do they ever remember the Tabernacle? Do they spend their days and nights at the foot of the altar pouring forth their souls in love and gratitude to Jesus in the Blessed Sacrament? Alas, far from it! Thine altars, O loving Jesus, are lonely and Thy churches deserted. The canticles of the angels of the tabernacle alone ascend before Thy throne.

The blessed spirits of Heaven pay due homage to our Saviour, while men forget Him. Yet it was not for angels but for men that Jesus lived and died; it is for men alone that Jesus, in His mercy and love, remains day and night on our altars. Oh, how ungrateful are we who think so little of the Sacred Heart of Jesus burning with Divine love for us in the tabernacle! Most holy Heart of Jesus, inspire us with a true spirit of reparation, and warm and fill our cold hearts with love for Thee!

Our Lord Himself Prescribes the Manner of Atonement

It is very remarkable that Our Lord, in introducing the devotion to His Sacred Heart, pointed out the way in which atonement should be made. Thus He selected the day on which the Feast of His Sacred Heart should be celebrated. "I demand," He said to St. Margaret Mary, "that the first Friday after the Octave of Corpus Christi be made a special festival in honor of My Sacred Heart by receiving Holy Commu-

nion on that day, and by making reparation of honor, in atonement for the insults
and outrages perpetrated against My Heart
while exposed on the altar."

Previously, He had given His servant a
similar command. Once when she was
kneeling before the Blessed Sacrament
exposed, He showed her His Sacred Heart
and said: "Hearken to what I request of
thee. Thou shalt receive Me in Holy Communion as often as obedience permits thee.
. . . thou shalt communicate every first Friday of the month. . . ."

Thus did our Saviour expressly declare
that it is *by the reception of Holy Communion that He desires to see His Sacred Heart
honored.* It might be objected that His command was meant only for St. Margaret
Mary, or that we are not bound to receive
Holy Communion on the Feast of the Sacred
Heart or on the First Friday of the month.
True, we are not bound to do so under pain
of sin, but it is likewise true that the Communion of Reparation, when made on these
days, is the most pleasing, the most acceptable and therefore the most sublime practice of devotion to the Sacred Heart, and
whosoever receives Holy Communion thus

may rest assured that he gives great pleasure to the Sacred Heart of Jesus.

That the invitation to receive the Communion of Reparation on these days is also meant for *us* follows clearly from Our Lord's words: "And I promise that My Heart shall open wide to pour out plentifully the influence of Its love upon all those who shall give such honor to It, or cause it to be given."

When Should the Communion of Reparation Be Received?

The First Friday of the month is dedicated to the Sacred Heart of Jesus and is therefore called *Sacred Heart Friday*. Friday, in general, takes an important part in the empire of grace. We need but consider Good Friday. *Our Lord also chose Friday for the Communion of Reparation*. But if it is impossible to receive Holy Communion on that day, we should do so on Sunday or on some other day of the week, taking care to form the intention to make reparation and render atonement and to rejoice the Heart of our Saviour. The following formula may be used, although one may also make the intention in one's own words:

"My dearest Lord Jesus, I will now receive this Holy Communion for love of Thee, in atonement for all the coldness and for all the sins whereby mankind has ever offended Thee in the Sacrament of Thy Love."

How pleasing to the Sacred Heart of Jesus will this pure intention be! Surely it will merit for you the fulfillment of His loving words: "I will be thy refuge during life, and above all in death."

The Great Promise

With regard to the pious practice of the Communion of Reparation on the First Friday of the month, Our Lord made a promise that far surpasses, in magnanimity, all the others and is therefore called the *Great* Promise. It reads as follows:

"I promise thee, in the excessive mercy of My Heart, that My all-Powerful love will grant to all those who communicate (receive Holy Communion) on the First Friday of the month, for nine consecutive months, the grace of final penitence; they shall not die in My displeasure nor without their Sacraments; My Divine Heart shall be their refuge in this last moment."

Is this not a great, a wonderful promise? Pious and devout men consider it a most marvelous favor, the most precious promise of the Sacred Heart. It is not, of course, an *article of faith;* it is merely a revelation to St. Margaret Mary, by means of which Our Lord wished to introduce into the world the devotion to His Divine Heart. But the credibility of these promises may be concluded from the holy, irreproachable life of St. Margaret Mary, from the examination made by ecclesiastical authorities, from the blessings which the devotion to the Sacred Heart has diffused over the world, and from the sanction of the Church.

Of What Does the Great Promise Assure Us?

The promise is threefold. First, those who fulfill the *required conditions* are assured of the grace of *final perseverance,* that is, the grace to die in the love and friendship of God (that is, in the state of Sanctifying Grace). Should they have the misfortune to fall into mortal sin, they will have the grace to repent before being called out of this world.

Secondly, it includes the grace *not to die*

without receiving the Sacraments. The promise says expressly: "They shall not die without receiving their Sacraments," that is to say, those Sacraments which are necessary for them to die well. To the just is promised the grace of perseverance; to the sinner, the grace of repentance; therefore, the usual means for attaining this grace, namely, the Sacrament of Penance (Confession), or Extreme Unction (Last Anointing), or at least perfect contrition, is also included.

Thirdly, the Divine Heart will be their *secure refuge* in the hour of death. When once the shadows of death surround the faithful Christian who has devoutly made the nine First Fridays, the Heart of Jesus will gratefully remember the sacrifices he has made and the joy he has given Him by his Communions of Reparation. The Sacred Wound of the side of our Saviour will be for him then a haven of peace; and the poor, anxious child of earth will pass securely through the valley of death, to rest forever in the Sacred Heart.

But do not say: "Very well, I will make the nine First Fridays, then I am perfectly certain of going to Heaven, no matter what kind of a life I may live."

No, Christian soul, it was not meant that way. Would this not be to sin presumptuously against God's mercy? The Church teaches that no one can say with infallible and absolute certainty that he will obtain the grace of final perseverance, unless this has been especially revealed to him. But if you have worthily received the Communion of Reparation on the nine First Fridays, and have subsequently lived a good life, you may confidently expect that Our Lord will redeem His promise.

Conditions of the Great Promise

Anyone wishing to participate in this marvelous favor must receive Holy Communion on the First Friday of the month for nine consecutive months. That the Communion must be received *worthily* (in the state of grace) goes without saying.

"But," you may ask, "would it not do just as well to receive the nine Communions of Reparation on nine first *Sundays* of the month? Is the promise restricted to the *First Friday?*"

The Sacred Heart is certainly infinitely good and will graciously accept your Communion of Reparation on Sunday or on any other day of the week. But in order to participate with certainty in the favor of the Great Promise, you must receive Holy Communion *on the First Friday,* the day appointed by Our Lord. No other day may be substituted.

Nor may the succession of the nine First Fridays be interrupted. In case you were to begin the nine Fridays and were on one Friday prevented from receiving Holy Communion, you would have to begin them over again.

Many persons may be obliged to make great sacrifices in order to comply with this condition. However, the promise of protection at the hour of death and the strong hope of life eternal will certainly give us courage for the greatest sacrifices and difficulties, as it did to a certain railroad employee who had to work regularly every week from Tuesday morning until Friday evening. Now what did this man do? He went to church to receive Holy Communion on Friday *evening.* He remained fasting all day until then.* He did this on nine First

---

* In the early 20th century, Church law required fasting from midnight from all food and drink, including

Fridays in succession. But the happiness and peace which he experienced on these First Fridays cannot be described.

God be praised, there are today many, a great many, souls who receive Holy Communion not only every First Friday, but even daily, or almost daily: souls for whom every Communion is a Communion of love, a Communion of Reparation. These souls have long since forgotten their own interests and now take delight only in the interests of Jesus, bitterly deploring the coldness and ingratitude of so many Christians. Oh, how inexpressibly great will be the reward of these noble souls on the great day of recompense.

---

water, before receiving Communion. Also, Mass was not permitted to be celebrated after twelve noon: so the railroad employee must have made a special request to a priest to give him Holy Communion outside of Mass.—*Publisher*, 2010.

Chapter 4

True Devotion and the Image of the Sacred Heart

IN order the better to realize the infinite love of the Son of God as manifested in the Incarnation, in His Passion and in the adorable Sacrament of the Altar, we need a *visible representation of this love.* Our Divine Saviour attached many graces and blessings to the veneration of the image of His adorable Heart.

Among the revelations which Jesus made to St. Margaret Mary concerning the various practices whereby He desires to be honored by men, one referred to the veneration of an image of His Sacred Heart. We may, therefore, say with truth that *the representation of the Divine Heart was desired by our Saviour Himself.* Let us hear the confidante of these marvelous revelations describe the vision during which were disclosed to her the essential outlines on which the image of the Sacred Heart of Jesus should be portrayed:

"One day, on the Feast of St. John the Evangelist, after having received from my Divine Saviour a favor similar to that bestowed upon the Beloved Disciple, of reposing on the bosom of Our Lord, the Divine Heart was represented to me on a throne of fire and flames, shedding on every side rays brighter than the sun and transparent as crystal. The Wound which He had received upon the Cross appeared there visibly; a crown of thorns encircled the adorable Heart, and It was surmounted by a cross.

"These instruments of His Passion signified, as my Divine Master gave me to understand, that it was His *unbounded love for man* which had been the source of all His sufferings. From the first moment of His Incarnation all these torments had been planted in His Heart. From that moment He accepted all the pains and humiliations which His Sacred Humanity was to suffer during the whole course of His mortal life, and even the outrages to which His love for man would expose Him till the end of time in the Blessed Sacrament. He revealed to me afterwards that it was the great desire of disclosing to mankind His Heart, and of giving them in these 'latter times' this last proof of His love, that induced Him to propose to them an object and a means so calculated to win their love. He opens to them His Sacred Heart with all the treasures of love, mercy and graces of sanctification and salvation which It contains."

Promises to Those Who Venerate The Image of the Sacred Heart

Our Divine Saviour assured St. Margaret Mary that He takes a singular pleasure in being honored under the representation of a heart of flesh, in order thereby to touch the insensible hearts of men.

As motives for venerating the image of His Sacred Heart, Our Lord proposes two in particular: first, the *blessings and graces* connected therewith; secondly, *the foundation of hope* in the distress of "latter times."

"For this," continues St. Margaret Mary, "He promised to pour into the hearts of all who would venerate His image the fullness of gifts with which His Sacred Heart abounds, saying that wherever this image would be exposed for special veneration, it would draw down upon the place every kind of blessing." Furthermore, He promised that all who would contribute to afford Him this joy would be blessed with graces of sanctification and salvation in superabundant measure. St. Margaret Mary wrote to a superior who caused the first picture of the Sacred Heart to be drawn: "For this service Our Lord will engrave your name in His Heart ineffaceably; the other rewards I am not permitted to reveal to you."

Flames Issuing from the Heart of Jesus

The sentiments which a picture of the Sacred Heart should incite in our souls may easily be inferred from the symbols with which our blessed Lord Himself wished to surround this image. First, the *flames* bursting forth and enveloping It show the vehement love wherewith It has loved and continually loves us. Our Lord exclaimed to St. Margaret Mary, "Behold this Heart that has loved men so much!" In order to conquer our indifference and to leave no excuse for ignorance, He discloses to us His Divine Heart, His longing desire being to inflame us with a grateful return of love. "Son, give Me thy heart!" is His pleading invitation to all.

From us the Heart of Jesus desires a practical love. Love is devotedness; it is a sacrificing of self. The world has grown cold and torpid in the love of God. For Jesus, there is no room anymore. To re-kindle our souls, to light up anew the flames of charity, Our Lord shows to the world His love-glowing Heart as a reminder of the greatness of His love. Truly, only the most heartless can resist such pleading.

Whenever we behold a picture of the Sacred Heart, let us make an act of love, saying with heart and lips: "O my Jesus, I love Thee, I give Thee my heart; give me Thy holy love!" A single act of love is of immeasurable merit. A single sigh of fervent love merits more than can be obtained through laborious work. St. Aloysius, by interior acts of love, rose in a short time to an astonishing degree of sanctity. Nothing dispels Satan more quickly when he tempts us than an efficacious act of love.

Hence, St. Francis de Sales advises us to make acts of love in time of temptation.

The Heart of Jesus Encircled With the Crown of Thorns

The crown of thorns encircling the Heart of Jesus typifies the injuries inflicted upon It by the ingratitude wherewith men requite His love. Nothing is more painful to a loving heart than to see its love despised. The greater the tokens of love received, the baser the ingratitude. From the crib to the Cross, what more could our compassionate Redeemer have done for us? Ah, His amiable Heart has loved us to excess, and as a supreme manifestation of His love and burning desire to remain with us, He instituted the wonderful Sacrament of the Altar. The Heart of Jesus wishes to become the food of our soul.

But alas, precisely in this Sacrament of Love, the most painful wounds are inflicted on His Sacred Heart! Hear His sorrowful complaint to the confidante of His Eucharistic sufferings: "Behold the Heart that has loved men so much that It has spared nothing, even to exhausting and consuming Itself, in order to testify to them

Its love. But in return I receive from the greater part of mankind only *ingratitude,* by reason of the contempt, irreverence, sacrilege and coldness shown Me in this Sacrament of Love. And what I feel still more painfully is that hearts consecrated to Me treat Me thus!"

Our Lord revealed the devotion to His Sacred Heart especially to obtain *reparation and atonement.* For this reason He appeared in the Sacred Host to St. Margaret Mary and united this devotion most intimately with devotion to the Blessed Sacrament. Those who venerate the Sacred Heart of Jesus should have great devotion to the Holy Eucharist. Our Lord desires especially the Communion of Reparation. Without reparation, devotion to His Sacred Heart would not be complete.

The Heart of Jesus Surmounted by a Cross

The Cross surmounting the Heart of Jesus is a further testimony of Our Lord's love for us; it reminds us particularly of His bitter Passion and Death. We cannot be devout clients of the Sacred Heart if we are unmindful of these tokens of His merciful goodness and love.

Many saints are represented holding a crucifix in their hands as a sign of their special devotion to the sufferings of Christ. Holy Church numbers among her saints more than 60 persons who bore the sacred stigmata in their body. Countless are the revelations of saints regarding the precious graces connected with devotion to the Passion of our Saviour. Our Lord once said to Blessed Angela of Foligno: "Those who seriously meditate on My Passion are in truth My children; the others are so in name only."

St. Augustine declares: "A single tear shed in remembrance of the sufferings of Christ is of more value than a pilgrimage to Jerusalem, or a year's fasting on bread and water, if it be not performed with the same love." On this account our Divine Saviour wishes the devotion to His Sacred Heart to be practiced especially on Fridays. On that day He gave the highest proof of His love, and we should make Him a return of love by patience in our sufferings. *Love for the Cross is the fruit of true devotion to the Sacred Heart.* The perfection of love consists in pure suffering. The way of the Cross leads to perfection. What grievous afflictions the Saints endured! They realized the infinite value of suffering.

The Wound of the Heart of Jesus

Devotion to the Heart of Jesus originated the moment when that Divine Heart was pierced with the lance. In this adorable Heart, touching mysteries lie hidden, the contemplation of which is most fruitful and abounding in grace. Various Fathers of the Church, among them the great St. Bernard, call special attention to the mysteries of the love of the Heart of Jesus manifested by Its being opened with a lance. During His whole life, our blessed Redeemer foresaw and desired this Wound in order to reveal His infinite love for man.

St. Margaret Mary understood this well, for when she drew the first little image of the Sacred Heart, she represented It with a gaping wound, in which she inscribed the word: "*Caritas.*" St. Frances of Rome relates that once she beheld the Wound of the Heart of Jesus, from which gushed forth a stream of living water. At the same time she heard these words: "I am Love crying aloud: 'If anyone thirsts, let him come to Me and drink.' I will satiate those who follow My invitation; it is just for this reason that I permitted My Heart to be pierced, that I might be able to receive all therein as in a place of refuge."

A remarkable passage of the *Apocalypse* which has been quoted as applicable to our times is "Behold, I have caused a door to be opened before thee, which no one can shut." (*Apoc.* 3:8). *The Wound of the Heart of Jesus is this wide-open door* of salvation for the whole world, this secure place of refuge for the most guilt-laden sinner; therein he may become white as snow. This Wound is a fountain of immeasurable grace and consolation. To those who venerate His Sacred Heart, our Divine Saviour imparts the Precious Blood and water which issued from His side, that they may offer It unceasingly to the Heavenly Father in expiation for their sins and those of the whole world. Through this offering we can obtain numberless graces for ourselves and others. We should, every morning, place our sufferings, prayers and labors in the pierced Heart of Jesus; there everything will be purified and perfected.

The Heart of Jesus Surrounded by Rays of Light

Rays of light always envelop representations of the Sacred Heart of Jesus. These rays, which dart in every direction, signify the great graces and blessings which emanate from devotion to the Sacred Heart. Most liberal are the promises made by Our Lord to those who venerate His Divine Heart. "Announce it, and let it be announced to the whole world," He revealed to St. Margaret Mary, "that I set neither limit nor measure to My gifts of grace for those who seek them in My Heart!"

This Divine Heart is a superabundant treasure house of all gifts of salvation. Any grace, howsoever exalted, we can hope to obtain from this adorable Heart. The Heart of Jesus is a boundless, fathomless abyss, an ocean at which thirsting and languishing humanity may refresh itself. Above all, poor sinners who take their refuge in the Heart of Jesus can there obtain true conversion. Our Lord revealed this devotion to His servant St. Margaret Mary in order to restore life to countless numbers and to save them from the clutches of Satan.

The Good Shepherd and Saviour is ever ready to remove the *heaviest burden,* to atone for the *blackest guilt.* He imparts torrents of grace to sinners who come to Him with confidence and humility. His joy at a real conversion is so great that He often grants graces to penitent sinners which He does not bestow on the innocent. Unspeakable graces are promised to those who *strive after sanctity.* St. Margaret Mary writes: "I know of no devotion better suited to lead a soul in a short time to the summit of perfection."

The Heart of Jesus is the *mine* and *treasure house* of graces. However, Our Lord promised not only spiritual favors to those who venerate His Heart, but also aid and comfort in all sufferings. No human soul, howsoever disconsolate and abandoned, will fail to find peace and consolation in the Divine Heart. No misfortune is so bitter and hopeless but that the Sacred Heart can change and direct it all for the best. O poor, afflicted human heart, whatever you can desire or crave for is contained superabundantly in the Heart of Jesus! O troubled, tried and abandoned human heart, whatever oppresses and agitates you may be confided to the Heart of your Friend, your Master and your King!

How Our Names Are Written In the Heart of Jesus

The great object of our Divine Lord's solicitude is devotion to His Sacred Heart. He would not have appeared so frequently to St. Margaret Mary, He would not Himself have instructed her in the minutest details of this devotion or made such magnanimous promises, had He not been most anxious that the veneration of His adorable Heart should be known and practiced. Therefore, He made a very consoling promise in favor of its promoters: *Those who propagate this devotion shall have their names written in My Heart, never to be blotted out.* Here He promises nothing less than the grace of final perseverance, the grace of predilection, of eternal happiness.

When the disciples had returned from their first mission journey, they related to Our Lord, full of joy, how they had performed miracles and driven out devils in His Name. But Our Lord told them not to rejoice on account of the evil spirits being subject to them, but because their names were written in Heaven.

What Our Lord designated as the greatest joy for His disciples, namely, the grace of predilection, He also promises to promoters of devotion to His Sacred Heart. "Their names shall be written in My Heart, never to be blotted out." Ah, let us not forget that we have no full security regarding our eternal salvation; the frightful uncertainty of eternal damnation ever exists. The more anxious we are to escape this everlasting misfortune, the more zealous we should be to look about for signs of predilection.

One of these signs, according to the doctrine of saints, is *veneration of Mary;* and another, according to the promise of Our Lord, is *zeal for spreading devotion to the Sacred Heart.* Devotion to the Sacred

Heart of Jesus is the devotion for our times; it is destined to heal the maladies of our age.

Let us fulfill Our Lord's desire; let us labor with all our strength for the spreading of devotion to the Sacred Heart of Jesus, and it will be a source of inexpressible consolation to us at the hour of our death.

Enthronement of the Sacred Heart

Every family ought to have a beautiful picture of the Sacred Heart in their home and, if possible, keep a light burning before it, at least on Fridays and on special feasts. The light might also be kept burning during novenas or for special intentions. This *childlike confidence in the Sacred Heart of Jesus is the key to the treasures of grace of this infinitely generous Heart.*

"I will bless every house where an image of My Heart is exposed and venerated," Our Lord promised to St. Margaret Mary. However, not until our own 20th century are the faithful beginning to realize the magnificence of this promise. God wishes to impress upon us the true meaning of these words. He has called an apostle to propagate in families a practice which has for its end the reign of the Sacred Heart in the home.

In 1910 Rev. Father Mateo, a South American missionary, was instantly cured of a hopeless malady in the sanctuary of Paray-le-Monial, where the Sacred Heart had appeared so often to St. Margaret Mary. At the time of his miraculous restoration to health, the pious priest felt inspired to devote his life to promoting devotion to the Sacred Heart, especially to realizing in families the graces attached to honoring the image. "I resolved," he said, "to gain family after family for the love of the Sacred Heart."

In many countries, including our own, he has preached his crusade of the *Enthronement,* that is, erecting an image of the Sacred Heart in the most honorable part of the house *as on a throne,* that Jesus may reign visibly in the family. Jesus must be the King of love and mercy, the Friend, the Counselor in every household. If He is permitted to exercise His dominion, He will banish from such homes the spirit of worldliness; fervor and devotion will flourish instead.

By the Enthronement of the Sacred Heart, the family is consecrated to the Heart of Jesus. Thereby the home becomes a sanctuary of God and is placed under the special protection of the Divine Heart. This protection is of inestimable value in all the joys and sorrows of the family. Jesus, full of love, is its very center. The children are brought up to consider as great, beautiful and noble only that which pleases the Divine Heart. They are trained to fear and to hate sin because it displeases the Sacred Heart, and the whole family is filled with great confidence in the loving, merciful Heart of Jesus. In Him it seeks secure refuge in all its trials.

Remarkable success has attended Father Mateo's efforts to spread this devotion. God has sanctioned his mission by miracles of grace; marvelous conversions have resulted from this apostolate. Pope St. Pius X and Popes Benedict XV, Pius XI and Pius XII have highly commended his work. These holy Pontiffs recognized in the Enthronement of the Sacred Heart a powerful means of establishing the dominion of the Sacred Heart in Christian families. Through this reign of the Divine Heart, our homes, the true foundation of the nation, will be preserved from the corruption of the wicked world.

Chapter 5

True Devotion
and Confidence

The Power of a Novena to the
Sacred Heart

ST. Gemma Galgani, a child of grace,
died on Holy Saturday, April 11, 1903.
She had been born on March 12,
1878, near Lucca, Italy, of thoroughly
Catholic parents who had met with many
misfortunes and reverses. When eight years
old, Gemma lost her excellent mother; soon
after the death of her father in 1897,
Gemma herself became seriously ill. She
suffered from tuberculosis of the spine,
alarming attacks of meningitis, total loss
of hearing and paralysis of the limbs. Doc-
tors employed all their skill in her behalf,
but the malady grew daily worse.

Confined to her bed of pain, Gemma
could no longer move her limbs and was
entirely dependent upon the charitable aid

of others. In this painful condition she passed many weary months, with no other comfort than prayer and resignation to the will of God. Her disease continued unchecked, and it soon became apparent that the end was near. On February 2, 1899, she received Holy Viaticum. It was feared she would not live until evening, and her friends bade her a last farewell.

Everybody was convinced that the patient sufferer was beyond the aid of human skill; only the intervention of Heaven could bring relief. One visitor brought Gemma the biography of Venerable Gabriel of Our Lady of Sorrows, of the Order of Passionists, who had died in the odor of sanctity in 1862. Pope Leo XIII, who declared this youthful saint "Venerable," called him "the Aloysius of the 19th century." Gabriel was canonized by Pope Benedict XV on May 13, 1920.

The biography of St. Gabriel at once inspired Gemma with confidence. She later declared: "That same evening I began to read the life of Venerable Gabriel, and I did not weary of taking it up again and again and admiring his virtues and example. Thenceforth I felt a special devotion to him. I felt his presence near me. In all my actions, the Venerable Gabriel was in my thoughts." Gabriel was in truth near Gemma, and he called her "sister."

A religious then advised Gemma to make a novena to St. Margaret Mary Alacoque for a complete cure or for the grace of entering Heaven immediately after death. To please the good Sister, Gemma began the novena on February 23, 1899. Let us again hear Gemma's own words: "It was but a few minutes before midnight when I heard the rustling of a rosary and felt a hand laid on my forehead. It was Venerable Gabriel. Then I heard a voice repeating nine times in succession the *Pater, Ave* and *Gloria*.

"Through sheer weakness I could scarcely answer. The voice then asked me, 'Wilt thou be healed? Pray with faith to the Sacred Heart of Jesus every evening. I will come daily as long as the novena lasts, and we will pray together to the Sacred Heart.' And he really came every evening, laying his hand on my forehead while we recited the prayers to the Sacred Heart of Jesus, adding, by his desire, three times the *Gloria Patri* in honor of Blessed

Margaret Mary. The novena ended on the First Friday of March."

The time had arrived when Gemma's great patience was to be rewarded. She was not to die; God intended to glorify her by the fullness of His most extraordinary gifts before taking her to Himself. But in order that she might be delivered from her frightful sufferings, a great miracle was required. This miracle Our Lord in His mercy and goodness was pleased to perform.

At the close of the novena to the Sacred Heart, Gemma sent for her confessor and made her Confession. After Holy Communion, Jesus said to her, "Gemma, wilt thou be cured?" Overcome with emotion, she answered only with her heart: "As Thou wilt, my Jesus."

Gemma was restored to health: her cure was as complete as it was instantaneous. Scarcely had two hours passed when she arose. The relatives and members of the household wept with joy. She now received Holy Communion again daily, for she had a consuming desire for this heavenly Food. Three months after her cure, she received the sacred stigmata. During the four years that she still lived, wonderful mysteries were imparted to her, such as have been imparted only to the greatest saints. Since her death God has glorified her through miracles. She was canonized by Pope Pius XII on May 2, 1940.

Aid through the Sacred Heart of Jesus

Oh, how great, how inexhaustible are the hidden treasures of the Sacred Heart of Jesus! In this most loving Heart the Saints of every age reposed in peace. In the Sacred Heart they found consolation, nay, joy, in trials and sufferings; courage to fight the battles of the Church; and new motives every day to live, to labor, to suffer and to shed their blood for the glory of God, their own sanctification and the salvation of souls.

The Sacred Heart of Jesus is the boundless ocean of God's love, of God's mercy, of God's tender compassion for poor sinners. The Sacred Heart of Jesus contains remedies for all our wants, and It can and will supply all our needs for time and eternity. In our troubles, in our sorrows, in our wants, let us not forget to go to that place where alone we can find peace, consolation and help—the Sacred Heart of Jesus!

Our Divine Saviour invites especially the suffering, those who are heavily afflicted, to take refuge in His Sacred Heart. No favor is so great but that it can be obtained from the Sacred Heart of Jesus; no human soul is so desolate and abandoned but that this Divine Heart can fully console and gladden it; no misfortune is so great and hopeless but that the Heart of Jesus can change and direct everything for the best. In whatever manner the human heart is oppressed and troubled, it will find aid in the Heart of Jesus. "Come to me, all you who labor and are burdened, and I will give you rest." (*Matt.* 11:28).

Countless are the favors that have been granted through novenas to the Sacred Heart! If you, dear reader, are in trouble or affliction, implore the Sacred Heart of Jesus, and It will come to your aid likewise, in the way that is best for you and your salvation.

A most commendable practice is to receive Holy Communion devoutly during or at the end of the novena. The devotions may be held before a picture of the Sacred Heart if this can well be done, for Our Lord attached great blessings to the devout veneration of the image of the Sacred Heart. A suitable time for making a novena would be especially the days preceding the First Friday of the month; thereby they would become truly a novena of grace for all.

Confidence, the Key to the Heart of Jesus

St. Margaret Mary calls confidence *the key to the Heart of Jesus.* When our Divine Saviour still walked on earth, healing the sick and performing other miracles for suffering humanity, He generally asked those who sought aid whether they had faith and confidence. Not until they answered, "Lord, I believe," or gave a similar expression of faith did He speak the word of omnipotence. By this He meant to teach us that in prayer, *faith and confidence are the paramount conditions.*

The petitioner may measure the greatness of his favor by the degree of his confidence. If you go to the well to fetch water, how much do you draw? With a small vessel, a small quantity; with a large one you carry a great deal. Centuries ago the holy Doctor of the Church, St. Cyprian, declared:

"The deeper our vessel of confidence, the greater will be the abundance of the heavenly waters of grace."

St. Gertrude once asked Our Lord what she ought to do to obtain a certain favor. His answer was: "Confidence alone can easily obtain everything!" And again: "Although I regard with pleasure all that is done for My glory, as prayers, fasts, vigils and other like works of piety, yet *the confidence with which the elect have recourse to Me* in their weakness *touches Me far more sensibly.*" We must especially not lose confidence if our requests are not immediately granted. Often the Sacred Heart desires several novenas. A confiding soul's perseverance in prayer will never be confounded.

Chapter 6

True Devotion And Union

OUR prayers, works and sufferings have an eternal value only when united to the merits of Jesus Christ. "Without Me you can do nothing." From the revelations of saints we may infer how ardently our Saviour desires us to live in union with Him.

Holding His Heart in His hand, Jesus once said to St. Gertrude: "Behold My most magnificent Heart, the melodious harp whose notes ravish the Holy Trinity. I give It to thee, and as a faithful and diligent servant It will be at thy disposal to supply for all thy powerlessness."

Atonement. Our Saviour addressed similar words to St. Margaret Mary. Pleading for her reparation to make amends for the rejection of His Sacred Heart by mankind,

Jesus said: "Do thou at least give Me the consolation of supplying for their ingratitude." He speaks the same words to us, and, like the humble Visitandine, we too complain of our inability. Alas, how can we render worthy reparation? How can we give the Sacred Heart true consolation? Jesus has given us a way. Opening His Heart to us as to His blessed confidante, He exclaims: "See, this will enable you to supply all your deficiencies." Yes, our Divine Lord gives us His all-powerful Heart as a means to offer atonement.

Love. Inspired by Our Lord, St. Margaret Mary often repeated: "Eternal Father, I offer Thee the most pure love and the ardent desires of the Sacred Heart of Jesus in satisfaction for my cold and tepid love."

Thanksgiving. And again, she prayed: "Heavenly Father, behold the adorable Heart of Thy beloved Son, which I present to Thee in thanksgiving for all the graces and benefits Thou hast bestowed upon me."

Good works. It was revealed to St. Gertrude that all the graces which come from Heaven to earth pass through the adorable Heart of Jesus. It is the same with our works: To be acceptable to the Eternal Father, everything must be purified in the Heart of His Son (or that of our Heavenly Mother). The Sacred Heart of Jesus is our *altar;* let us place our *actions* and *sacrifices* on It to be rendered worthy of the Blessed Trinity. "Make use of My Heart, and thy deeds will charm the eye and ear of the Divinity," Jesus told St. Gertrude. "I know thy weakness," He continued. "My Heart is ever ready to repair thy defects and shortcomings. It desires with incredible ardor to do so. All I ask is that thou confide to Me all thy care, if not by words, at least by some movement of thy will."

Faults. St. Gertrude understood how the Heart of Jesus makes satisfaction for our faults. When she humbled herself for her negligences, Our Lord poured forth on her from His Sacred Heart all the virtue and beauty of His Divine perfections, which concealed her imperfections from the Divine Goodness. Speaking to St. Margaret Mary, He called His Heart the "source of all healing and sanctifying graces."

"Give Me thy heart," Jesus asks of us as of St. Gertrude. Let us give it to Him; let us live this life of union so glorious for God, so sweet and fruitful for our souls, so powerful for us to obtain graces for our brethren. In the Sacred Heart our *prayers* will be sanctified, our *atonement* rendered acceptable, our *love* purified, our *thanksgiving* enhanced, our *good works* ennobled, our *faults* supplied for.

Our Lord most earnestly craves for this interior union of our soul with Him. He has indicated this to a latter-day confidante of His Heart, Mother Mary of the Divine Heart, a Good Shepherd religious, who died in the odor of sanctity but a few years ago. "He (Our Lord) declares," said this venerable nun, "that since the exterior cultus of His Divine Heart has been introduced by His apparitions to St. Margaret Mary and is known everywhere, He desires now that the interior cultus be established, that is to say, that *souls grow in the habit of uniting themselves interiorly ever more and more with Him,* offering Him their hearts as His abode." Mother Mary of the Divine Heart also said, "The

Heart of Jesus hungers and thirsts and desires to embrace the whole world in Its love and mercy."

Promises of the Sacred Heart to St. Margaret Mary for Those Who Honor His Sacred Heart

1. I will give them all the graces necessary for their state in life.
2. I will establish peace in their families.
3. I will comfort them in their trials.
4. I will be their secure refuge during life and, above all, in death.
5. I will shed abundant blessings on all their undertakings.
6. Sinners will find in My Heart an infinite ocean of mercy.
7. Lukewarm souls will become fervent.
8. Fervent souls will rapidly grow in holiness and perfection.
9. I will bless every place where an image of My Heart shall be exposed and honored.
10. I will give to priests the gift of touching the most hardened hearts.
11. The names of those who promote this devotion will be written in My Heart, never to be blotted out.

12. I promise thee, in the excessive mercy of My Heart, that My all-powerful love will grant to all those who receive Holy Communion on the First Friday of nine consecutive months, the grace of final penitence; they shall not die in My disgrace nor without receiving their Sacraments; My Divine Heart shall be their safe refuge in this last moment.

Chapter 7

Prayers

Daily Oblation in Union With the Eucharist

O LORD Jesus Christ, in union with that Divine intention with which Thou didst on earth offer praises to God through Thy Most Sacred Heart, and dost now continue to offer them in all places in the Sacrament of the Eucharist and will do so to the end of the world, I most willingly offer Thee, throughout this entire day, all my intentions and thoughts, all my affections and desires, all my words and actions, in imitation of the most Sacred Heart of the Blessed Virgin Mary ever Immaculate.

O SWEETEST Heart of Jesus, I implore that I may ever love Thee more and more.

Morning Offering
Through the Heart of Mary

O DIVINE Heart of Jesus, through the compassionate Heart of Mary, I offer Thee all the prayers, all the works and all the sufferings of this day, to atone for all the offenses committed against Thee. All this I offer in accord with the intentions Thou dost constantly have at Thy Sacrifice on the Altar.

Prayer to Return God's Love

B EHOLD, O my most loving Jesus, to what an excess Thy boundless love has carried Thee! Of Thine own Flesh and Precious Blood Thou hast made ready for me a Divine Banquet in order to give me all Thyself. What was it that impelled Thee to this transport of love? Nothing else, surely, but Thy most loving Heart. O adorable Heart of my Jesus, burning furnace of Divine Love, within Thy most Sacred Wound receive Thou my soul, that in that school of charity I may learn to requite the love of that God who has given me such wondrous proofs of His love. Amen.

A Novena to the
Sacred Heart of Jesus

(To be prayed with great confidence.)

O DIVINE Jesus, Who hast said, **"Ask and you shall receive; seek and you shall find; knock and it shall be opened unto you,"** behold me prostrate at Thy feet. Animated with a lively faith and confidence in these promises dictated by Thy Sacred Heart and pronounced by Thine adorable lips, I come to ask *(here mention your request)*.

From whom shall I **ask,** O sweet Jesus, if not from Thee, Whose Heart is an inexhaustible source of all graces and merits? Where shall I **seek,** if not in the Treasury which contains all the riches of Thy clemency and bounty? Where shall I **knock,** if it be not at the door of Thy Sacred Heart, through which God Himself comes to us and through which we go to God?

To Thee, then, O Heart of Jesus, I have recourse. In Thee I find consolation when afflicted, protection when persecuted, strength when overwhelmed with trials, and light in doubt and darkness. I firmly believe that Thou canst bestow upon me the grace I implore, even though it would require a miracle. Thou hast only to will it, and my prayer is granted. I admit that I am most unworthy of Thy favors, O Jesus, but this is not a reason for me to be discouraged. Thou art the God of Mercy, and Thou wilt not refuse a contrite and humble heart. Cast upon me a look of pity, I implore Thee, and Thy compassionate Heart will find in my miseries and weakness a pressing motive for granting my petition.

But, O Sacred Heart, whatever may be Thy decision with regard to my request, I will never cease to adore, praise and serve Thee. Deign, my Jesus, to accept this my act of perfect submission to the decrees of Thine adorable Heart, which I sincerely desire may be fulfilled in me and by me and by all Thy creatures forever and ever. Amen.

Holy Aspirations

O SACRED Heart of Jesus, Thy Kingdom come.

EUCHARISTIC Heart of Jesus, increase in us faith, hope and charity.

HEART of Jesus, burning with love of us, inflame our hearts with love of Thee.

O DIVINE Heart of Jesus, convert sinners, save the dying, free the holy souls in Purgatory.

Offering of the
Love of the Sacred Heart
By St. Margaret Mary

ETERNAL Father, I offer Thee the most pure love and the ardent desires of the Sacred Heart of Jesus in satisfaction for my cold and tepid love. Amen.

Offering of the Sacred Heart
In Thanksgiving
By St. Margaret Mary

HEAVENLY Father, behold the adorable Heart of Thy beloved Son, which I present to Thee in thanksgiving for all the graces and benefits Thou hast bestowed upon me. Amen

Prayer before Receiving
Holy Communion in Reparation

MY dearest Lord Jesus, I will now receive this Holy Communion for love of Thee, in atonement for all the coldness and for all the sins whereby mankind has ever offended Thee in the Sacrament of Thy Love. Amen.